A DAUBER'S
PROGRESS

Hank Adlam

ARROWSMITH

By the same Author:
On and Off the Flight Deck, published by Pen & Sword Aviation
Life is a Yo-Yo, published by Arrowsmith

A Dauber's Progress
first published in Great Britain in 2012 by
Arrowsmith
34 Hill Grove
Bristol BS9 4RQ

ISBN 978-0-9562919-2-9

A CIP catalogue record for this book is
available from the British Library.

Cover photographs by Heather and Aza Adlam
Typesetting by the Publisher
Scanning, cover and production by 4Word, Bristol

A Dauber's Progress

IN my dictionary daubing is described as, 'the laying of colour on a canvas roughly and crudely to form a picture'. Well, that's what I do and have been doing as a relaxation for many years past whenever work and opportunity has allowed. And what enormous fun, pleasure and excitement it has given me. Daubing is really a form of Do It Yourself painting and offers a whole new range of possibilities for those who have always yearned to paint pictures of lovely scenes and happenings or even people. It is for those who foolishly tell themselves that they have no draughtsmanship, cannot sketch and have no knowledge of how to mix and use paints. What nonsense. So long as you have pictures in your mind, which thrill and excite you, you can daub them with oil paints on canvas or board and this becomes tantamount to painting.

I have always firmly believed that if you want to learn a new activity or skill, then eschew the classroom and the ponderous pundits and for heaven's sake get on and have a go at it by yourself. Painting lends itself particularly well to this creed because it is so natural to begin as a DIY dauber and, if the pictures in your mind are strong enough, you will gradually and surely develop your own method of painting them. I realise that some art forms, such as music for one example, and other skills, require to be taught right from the start, but painting isn't one of them. This little book is all about the fun of teaching oneself how to paint landscapes and seascapes or indeed anything else, other than portraits and still life. I exclude these last two because they both require the skill of trained draughtsmanship. My book is for those who, like me, cannot abide the prospect of sitting among a group of people, all assiduously trying to paint the same probably boring object, which has been chosen and set in front of them by a teacher. I reckon that such students are missing all the excitement of discovering for themselves the pleasure at each stage of learning to paint.

I regret so much that I didn't start to daub until I was thirty-four and I deplore those earlier years when I wasted leisure time which could have been spent daubing. The reason for such a late start stems from my boyhood when at fourteen years old I was boarding at Harrow school. At the time I was interested only in playing games such as rugby and cricket, yet for some reason I decided to attend voluntary classes in art, which were offered once a week outside the usual curriculum. The art master was a small pot-bellied and bald little man who insisted that we start by learning a form of writing called copperplate in which I had no interest whatsoever. Eventually, towards the end of the second lesson, he placed an object which looked like a pot of some sort on a tall stand in the middle of the classroom. We were told to make a drawing of the thing with the paper and pencil provided on our desks. Well, what boy of fourteen wants to draw a po, for heaven's sake? Had he put a model of an aeroplane, a car or a yacht maybe, that would have been fun to try to draw for the first time. On my desk was this lovely large sheet of thick white drawing paper and it was irresistible. I made it into a super dart and, waiting until the master was looking the other way, sent it zooming across the room towards my friend at the far side. But it developed a steep turn and swerved towards that idiotic pot and clipped it as it sped past, just as the master turned in time to see what was happening. He, humourless little man, didn't waste any time but went straight to a cupboard, seized a cane, ordered me to bend over the desk and beat me hard on my bottom. As a silly schoolboy, sore of bottom and sore of mind at the unfairness of having been punished during a voluntary class, I vowed never again to attend an art class or to take any interest in art.

Twenty years later, at Christmas with our two young children, my wife gave me a present off the tree of a child's set of 'painting by numbers'. It was our family custom to give simple childish presents off the tree in addition to our more thoughtful grown-up presents, carefully wrapped and placed around the foot of the tree. It wasn't until the late evening, after our children, tired after all the excitements of the day, had gone to bed that I looked at the painting set. It contained several little tubes of different-coloured oil paint, including a much larger tube of white for some reason, together with pages of linen-type paper and a couple of small brushes. Vaguely amused at myself for doing so, I started to play with the set of paints and became absorbed as I messed and mixed them about on the linen paper. I was entranced with the effects as the paints merged.

I could hardly wait until the end of the school holidays to attempt an actual painting and I formed in my mind a picture of a typical Irish cottage with mountains behind based on our previous summer holiday in the west of Ireland. The ground around the cottage would surely be green, so I spread most of the little tube of green paint on the lower half of the linen page and, hovering over this green area, I put a vertical stick of brown paint with a yellow top on it to represent a tree and next to it a blob of yellow ochre as the cottage. I filled in the rest with some paler green for the mountains and there it was, my first daub! I realised how awful it was and that either of my two children, at ages five and six, could have done much better, but yet I was absurdly pleased with it and myself. Undaunted at the absurdity of it, a day later I had a go at painting a Seascape. When finished, you could tell it was a seascape by the child-like sailing boat hovering in the air above a dark blue area for the sea, which had some black rocks on it. The following morning being a Saturday, I made the first of many visits to an art shop where I bought loads of different colour paint tubes, bigger brushes, a palette and linen-covered boards on which to do my daubs. For months, almost every evening until well into the early morning hours, I daubed like a maniac and filled board and canvas with scene after scene. Often I scrapped the rubbish picture I had completed and re-daubed another on top of the mess I had made. But as a dauber, I was learning fast and getting better ... much better. Not for me the dreaded art class: I refused to study under a famous artist because I had seen how his pupils all painted in his particular style. Instead I visited art galleries, museums and exhibitions to study paintings which impressed me, and tried to see how and why the artist had painted in that particular manner. It must have been a relief to my family when, after that first frantic period of painting every evening late into the night, I settled down to just enjoy daubing like a normal chap whenever work and time allowed.

In the following years, we took our family holidays whenever we could on the west coast of Ireland, where I was inspired by the rugged and wild beauty of the mountainous area known as the Twelve Pins. I could imagine a dinosaur, or other such beast from thousands of years ago, roaming among the valleys of dark peat and rocks in the shadows of those little mountains with their tops hidden in the menacing skies above. What a wonderful country it was for a dauber to explore. Also we would spend our time on the coast itself where we could park our caravan in splendid isolation among miles and miles of sand dunes and empty beaches facing a brilliant blue sea. A perfect playground for family and daubers alike. As a dauber I owe much to the wild beauty of Ireland and to the impetus it gave me to try and capture in paint the mood and mystical feel of the land.

During that time my daubs, which had been the result of my self-teaching and study of work by real artists, had improved, and I was able to sell them, mainly to my friends to begin with. As word of my improving talents went the rounds, I started to sell to their acquaintances as well. Gradually the art gallery in Belfast, and one in Dublin, began to accept them for sale at prices sufficient to cover the cost of my daubing materials. In 1958 I was persuaded by a friendly professional artist to submit a picture for the annual exhibition by the Royal Ulster Academy and, with a dauber's luck; it was not only accepted but sold. Later, I was elected a member of the Academy.

A DAUBER'S PROGRESS

To those of you who are still convinced that you don't have any of the skills with which to paint, please let me tell you that you almost certainly do have those skills, buttoned up inside those convictions, but you may need a few tips on how to release them. To paint a picture I think that you need a feeling for the beauty and excitement of the world around you and the yearning to demonstrate that feeling pictorially. As for the means and skills of painting, these are not as difficult to find as they are made out to be, and they are available to most of us under the name of daubing. Your ambition as a dauber should be firstly to enjoy daubing and secondly that the daub should please and satisfy you when it is completed. If it also gives pleasure to others, perhaps to the point that they want to buy it, then what more could you want? If your first efforts appear to be as appallingly bad as mine did, look carefully and you may find something good and hopeful about them.

In any event don't be daunted, get cracking and daub some more.

On the assumption that you have not painted a picture before and you are now keen to start, I have described in the following pages what I have discovered and learned while getting on with daubing under my own steam. I hope that you may pick up some useful tips from my descriptions, and from some examples of my daubs. I do not believe that one can be taught pictorial art by another person because such art is related to our personal feelings and experience. Therefore it doesn't help if someone tries to tell us in a classroom what to paint and how to paint it. On the other hand, getting a tip from a fellow dauber can be valuable, whether from studying his or her paintings or in discussion over a glass of beer in a pub. You will find that most daubers are happy to share their knowledge, although some of those who regard themselves as serious Artists are not so forthcoming. In any event, I don't believe we should take pictorial art too seriously, especially now in a period when the professional art critics acclaim a sleazy bed, a dead sheep and a pile of bricks as great art! To be fair, perhaps these were a way, if not a very artistic one, of showing us how squalid is life for some, how inevitable is death and how uncomfortable it is to be constipated. How can we possibly take such nonsense seriously, unless perhaps the Artists are telling us that much of modern art is entirely bogus and that we should regard their works as no more than a bit of fun?

Painting mediums, or: What sort of paint to use?

I have defined a dauber in preceding pages as one who has little or no draughtsmanship or previous painting experience. If that is so, then I must begin by suggesting that Watercolours, although they give such beautiful and subtle effects, are not for you as a dauber. They are too difficult to use and require a natural gift of draughtsmanship. If you make a mistake at any stage with a watercolour painting, there is little possibility of correcting it and all you can do is scrap it and start again with a fresh page.

Acrylic paints are easier but they also require good draughtsmanship and, anyway, the resulting picture so often looks dead, like a poster, and rarely gives lasting pleasure.

No, the only painting medium for you, as a Dauber, is Oil.

Tools of the trade

There are all sorts of things you can use for putting the paint on to the canvas but I think the most important in this order are: firstly a big brush, then your fingers, a broad daubing knife, a fan brush (the bristles are spread out in the shape of an open fan), two smaller brushes, one very fine brush, little stick things with cotton wool ends (normally used to clean your ears out), a plastic knife for mixing the paints on the palette and some charcoal sticks. If you can't afford to use canvas, hardboard with a covering of either linen or gesso will do.

Most important is a nice big brush about three fingers wide, which is all you need for sploshing the paint (daubing) on most of the canvas while, for more detailed areas, the corner edges of the brush can be used. Two other smaller brushes may be needed and I suggest to fellow daubers to use a fan brush, which is good for daubing grass or tree branches and stuff like that. Daubers don't need to mix oil and turps any more as there is an excellent replacement called Liquin™. Wooden palettes have long gone out and are replaced by paper palettes, which are much better and don't need cleaning. Those little sticks with cotton wool at the ends are awfully good for nicking off little bits of paint on areas of the canvas where they shouldn't be. Most important for daubing are your fingers with which you can help to shape objects and also delicately lighten or darken them. Charcoal sticks are needed with which to sketch a few thin lined of composition on to the virgin canvas. If new daubers are concerned that modern paints out of a tube may not last as long as those mixed in the olden days by the artist himself, well, they may not, but I can say that one of my daubs, which I did and sold fifty years ago, looks as clear and bright as it has ever done.

I am not a camera

In a strange way my inability to draw or sketch any object which I see in front of me has been a blessing because it prevented me at the outset from copying. So many novice daubers, pleased by a colourful photograph or postcard, begin their daubing career by trying to copy the photo and, although doing so may eventually improve their ability to sketch, copying will never develop their imagination or their potential artistic sense. I recognise that the camera has a role to play in art, particularly in portraiture and painting children and animals as they never keep still enough to be sketched. I too use a camera but only to record details of a landscape such as an unusual type of rock, the shape of a group of trees, a derelict cottage maybe or even a telegraph pole. I am not interested in the camera's view of the landscape itself because that will be lodged in my own mind and memory to be arranged in due course as I want it into a picture for daubing.

Mixing and messing about with the paints

One of the lessons I learned from my first two daubs was that using basic colours straight out of the tube could never produce a realistic effect. Mixing the colours with white paint, as if it was water, made an obvious improvement but experiments of just mixing the various colours together didn't serve and I was at a stand on how to make any progress. Then came a breakthrough. I dislike plain blue skies in a picture because, in my lifetime as an aviation pilot, such skies seemed rarely to occur. But I discovered that by mixing almost any two strong colours together with white would produce greys of varying strength some of which were suitable as clouds. The best grey I found for that purpose, was white mixed with burnt umber and cobalt blue to give a strong grey while white mixed with light red and viridian green would produce a nice cool grey. This last grey incidentally, with a little burnt sienna and yellow ochre added, will make into a good flesh colour.

The breakthrough was to realise at last that either of those greys, mixed with other colours appropriate to the picture, is the basis of all daubing by giving the essential tone value to the colours throughout the picture. It is the basis of distance in a landscape or seascape and only in the immediate foreground is naked colour ever needed.

Composing a daub

'Oh, I like that landscape (or seascape), where is it exactly?' This is the inevitable question at an exhibition, which I dread!

How disappointing for the questioner if I try to explain that it isn't anywhere in particular and that it is a painting which stands on its own and is in itself a small world. It is not a copy of a camera's view or a representation of anything in particular. It is a product of my sense of art, such as it is, and has been formed entirely in my mind under the influence of the three Ms, which are …. Memory, Mood and 'Magination.

Memory. Whether my daubs be of a wartime scene with warships and aircraft, a landscape, a seascape, children on a beach, seas or clouds, they are all dependent on memory, which is the essential factor in any daub. For instance, I am unable to sketch people and children on a beach, nor can I copy a photograph of them and so I just have to memorise their figures and their particularly their attitudes. As a dauber like me, you are not able to paint such figures in detail, but as you represent them with fine lines of paint on to the canvas, your memory will guide your small brush into giving life to the figures.

Mood. The mood and 'feel' of the land or sea, which may have been mystical or awesome as you remember it, is very important. But your own mood also governs the type of daub. For instance, I can be quite jolly and daub happy beach scenes or even pretty little country cottages. Yet, more often, fear is the spur which dictates what I am going to daub and how I daub it. The sea, for example, has always frightened me ever since I was a small child and was run over by a large wave on a beach. I have never been able to swim and yet had to spend five wartime years flying single-engine aircraft over the sea, including ditching into it. So of course I am fearful of the sea and it shows in all my sea daubs, even those of rocks and the seashore.

I fear and dislike aircraft and flying, which has made life often awkward and difficult for me since

13

they were my profession, but such apprehension has spurred me to create daubs of wartime situations, which have been particularly sought after by airmen and ex-airmen.

I cannot abide pretty clouds. Whereas everyone can now fly cosseted throughout the journey by radar and automatic pilots, the weather in my flying days was a dominant factor, when to be in thick cloud with no means of knowing the ground below was fearful and fatal to many. Clouds have a magnificent grandeur but they are also full of menace and, in my opinion, there should always be a hint of their danger in every skyscape. Why is it that people, especially the young, walk about like zombies with horrible gadgets stuck into their ears and with their eyes all glazed and dead? They bumble about with eyes on the ground and rarely look up to see the great beauty of the sky above them.

Heights also terrify me and I cannot bear even to stand on a stool to change a light bulb, let alone climb a mountain. Hence I am mesmerised by mountains, which have such a majesty of their own, and so I like to include them in appropriate landscapes, but I have to look up at them as from ground level as I don't want to have to climb them. Other daubers, and artists too, paint in a mood of happiness and delight at the lovely colours of trees and flowers and, in time perhaps, they will come to abstract the stalks and just daub the strong colours and the shapes of flowers on their canvas. And why not, abstract art cuts out all the difficulty we daubers have with sketching, does it not?

'Magination. Imagination is the most vital of the three Ms and is the fire that can transform a potential ordinary painting into a great one. Imagination lights up the humdrum happenings and ordinary occasions to give excitement to a painting. It is imagination which makes just a painter, or even a dauber, into a true artist.

With imagination, for example, it is possible to bring a book to life by conveying its story onto canvas. I have attempted imaginative daubs of stories about ships of the Royal Navy in Nelson's time and in particular of the small fighting schooners, like HMS *Speedy* and HMS *Pallas* captained by Lord Cochrane, and HMS *Pickle* captained by Lapenotière. There is so much pleasure in imagining and daubing the weather and sea conditions for the picture and the consequent set of the sails, all that sort of thing. I found that researching the work of our trading ships and sailing trawlers during the nineteenth century provided many stories which could be made into imaginative daubing material, such as depicting the trading ships unloading their stores for the waiting villagers at rocky coves and beaches around the British Isles.

Imagination enabled me to illustrate stories for books and book covers. An ordinary-looking landscape can be made so much more interesting by adding a bit of this or that with imagination. Use what you see in front of you as the trigger. The enormous advantage of daubing with oil paints is that, when a mistake is made, it is so easy to scrape it out with a knife and this quite often results in a happy accident of bright mixed paint, which can be adapted imaginatively to improve the original idea of the picture. Once we get away from photographic views and use imagination instead, a whole new daubing world is opened.

Actual daubing: or sploshing the paint onto the canvas

There are no doubt many ways of doing this, but I am setting out my procedure in case any of it might be of help to new daubers.

First is to look at the virgin canvas and try to visualise onto it the picture you have in your mind. Take the charcoal stick and very lightly set out the basic position of the horizon and just a few main features of the composition.

As you look at the canvas, clarify in your mind where the focus point of your picture is going to be and think about the direction from which main light from the sky will come. Don't get into a tizzy about all this because, at the next stage when you are actually daubing, some of it may change, as happy accidents or just the way the painting is developing may encourage you to alter your original composition. No composition is set in stone and one of the joys of daubing sometimes is to follow where the paints lead you. Oh, and don't make a fuss about formal 'composition' as I believe they do in an art class and in arty books. Yes, the picture will be all the better if the dark and light areas in it are balanced and if the line of a road, for example, leads your eye to the focus point. But all that sort of thing is normal common sense allied to your own artistic sense. There is no need to make a big thing about it.

On the palette there should be two main big blobs of paint, one a tinted white and the other the mixed grey. Around these two major blobs place smaller quantities of various other colours including extra cobalt blue. Do the sky first. Plunge your big brush into the large tinted white blob and get lots of it with some Liquin on to the brush, which you next dip more gently into the grey mess. As you splosh all this up and down and side to side on to the top area of the canvas, you are in fact mixing your paints as you daub. The effect now should be a light sky with a darker grey area down at the horizon and a slightly bluer area at the top of the canvas because you also dipped the brush, which is thick with white already, into the cobalt blue for the purpose.

17

Now for the **clouds**. While the greyish-white stuff on the canvas is still wet, you re-dip the big brush into the tinted white but also this time you pick up more of the grey mess together with some more cobalt blue. You have to gauge how much of these on the white brush according to how dark you want the clouds to be. Merge the grey clouds into the light sky in whatever pattern you want, while remembering as you do so, that clouds, like everything else, have light and shadow in them. Isn't it fun? But although I write rather naughtily using words like 'stuff' and 'mess' about the paints on the palette, do please realise that oil paints are marvellous and, when you daub that 'mess' on to the canvas correctly, they will be lovely and you will be delighted.

If it is a **landscape** you are daubing then add other colours, such as burnt sienna, olive green, viridian, yellow ochre or whatever you want, into some of the already-mixed grey, which you have first lightened with the white. Using a clean big brush again, touch it into your chosen colours and mix each one on the brush with the grey foundation. These foundation colours can then be sloshed around the lower third of the canvas to form your landscape in accordance with the picture in your mind. Take care to put light on the land as you daub to accord with the light from your sky. The essence is that the further the distance, the more of the grey will be required in the colours. Whereas for instance on the immediate foreground you could daub some naked green and yellow colours as grass, bushes or whatever. When the daub is completed and dry, it might be that you find an item too strong for the distance in which it is placed. If that happens, my tip is that you mix a little bit of light blue grey and Liquin fluid, then kind of glaze it over the item, so that it becomes more distant.

Seascapes are rather more complicated because to start with you need to have studied and to know what the sea really looks like and how currents and wind shape it and the way it moves and breaks into waves. If you have never had any sea time, it is best for you and everyone else that you don't bother with seascapes. Or you could do what Turner, one of the greatest of all artists did: he deliberately spent time at sea and in very rough weather so that he knew something about the sea before he painted it. I should tell you that, as well as sailing small boats, I was at sea for some years in aircraft carriers and, when not flying, used to spend hours at a time just watching the sea and marvelling at its menacing power and majesty. Looking at a seascape, I can tell immediately whether the artist has ever had any real experience of the sea.

I so much regret that I do not have the artistry to portray the sea as strongly on canvas as I would like to do or remotely as well as some modern artists. Until the late 19th century, the sea was usually portrayed with symbolic curly blobs of white paint moving in orderly ranks like soldiers across the canvas. Then in the late 19th century and early 20th came some superb artists, from America as well as Britain, most of whom, having been professional sailors and trawler fishermen, knew their sea and how to portray it. In the mid 20th century came a whole bunch of absolutely brilliant modern seascape artists, some of whom are listed in a book by the Royal Society of Marine Artists with others who frankly are not all that good. My personal favourites are John Chancellor, Keith Shackleton and Geoff Hunt. These three have all had much sea time and have made the most of the great artistic gift they have been given by painting superbly realistic seascapes for us to enjoy. Though as daubers we may not be able to match their excellence, we need not feel all that far behind since very many of my simple seascapes have been acquired by people who evidently liked them. So it can be with any other new daubers reading this.

In a **seascape**, I may use three layers of paint for the sea itself. I start with masses of white paint tinted probably with viridian and, while I keep in mind that the sea direction is largely governed by the form and type of sky already painted, I spread this green tinted white stuff in swirls across the lower canvas using the big brush and my fingers. This first layer with heaps of white stuff is most important because I need to mould, yes mould, the shape and movement of the sea using a broad knife, my fingers and the large brush to do so. For example, I may squeeze and slurp the paint with my fingers into the shape of waves beginning to break at the top of a crested wave. I go on doing this and changing the shapes as I think fit, scraping parts out and re-doing them here and there, until I reckon it looks like the basis for the type of sea I want. Happy accidents sometimes occur during this process and, if so, take full advantage of them. The result is an impasto style of daubed paint but I leave an area of smooth white where I consider the sailing ship as my focus point will be placed. Then I go away from it for three days to allow this white mess to dry completely. If in a hurry for some reason, I put the canvas on a hot radiator or, if the canvas is small enough, I may put it in the hot oven for a short period, in a Delia Smith form of daubing. I might add that I normally have two or three daubs going at one time so that I can leave one or other for long periods to dry.

As a sort of P.S. to the above paragraph, I do realise that a new dauber may be horrified at reading my method of sploshing great blobs of paint about and then finger-daubing it around the canvas. Perhaps he or she might have heard a lecturer in a museum speak about the importance of delicate brushwork in a painting and believe it to be necessary. Codswallop, I say. I don't see how it matters a damn how you put the stuff on to the canvas, provided you succeed in creating the picture you wanted. It might be nice to paint with delicate brushwork and all that kind of thing, but I bet it isn't half as much fun and joyful as bashing it on as I do. In any case, it is a fair bet that all that delicate brushwork of a blue velvet gown or whatever was done by a boy apprentice rather than by the Great Master himself.

For the second layer of paint, I mix my usual grey, except that it should have more burnt umber than usual in it, with viridian, blue black and maybe some cobalt blue. It really is a matter of judgement for each of us as daubers to mix this mess about until it meets our idea of the dark area of that particular sea. When it looks about right, then spread it with varying strengths over the dry white stuff already on the canvas while keeping it quite wet with more Liquin than usual. This will enable the dark paint to be rubbed or thinned out with a finger to allow the white/viridian underneath to show through here and there as appropriate. New daubers will find all this to be good fun but messy and I recommend that the same jeans should always be worn when daubing so that you can continually wipe the paint off your fingers on them, as I do.

Now comes the really tricky and difficult business because we have to paint the basic shape of the boat's hull on to the selected smooth area of the sea. And we daubers can't draw, can we? I have tried to overcome my own lack of draughtsmanship in all sorts of ways, even by using tracing paper. But tracing doesn't serve and I can't be doing with all the paraphernalia of it, so I have to do the best I can with daubing the hull directly on to the canvas. At least I have the advantage of knowing what a ship at sea should look like and I have a clear and fairly precise picture of this one in my mind. Taking some of the already-mixed dark grey and using a quarter-inch pointed brush, I block in the basic shape of the hull but I make it a shade larger than I need. The reason for this is because in due course, when the hull is properly painted with final colour including its light and dark areas, I can make sure it is a correct shape by impinging the sea around the edges as I think necessary. Similarly with the mast and sails, I paint the surrounding sky around them and into the outside edges until they are correct. This daft-sounding procedure works for daubers like me who cannot draw well, although I have to admit that I have improved with practice over the past years.

The final painting of the sea is to put the lights and darks into the breaking waves and those around the area of the ship, which incidentally must be shown swimming well down in the sea and not sticking out of it like a sore thumb. I don't recommend, as I did for landscapes, the use of naked paint for the foreground of a sea and waves. On the contrary, these need all the more depth to them, which can be better shown with variations of grey and colour.

Aeroplanes and clouds

For a dauber who has difficulty in drawing, as I do, aircraft are a huge challenge because, as one example, the angle and dihedral of the wings with the main fuselage must be absolutely accurate. Again I have a small advantage having spent many years of my life as an aviator so I do at least know exactly what the aircraft should look like as it flies. But as for drawing the aircraft prior to daubing it … well, that is always a big problem for me. I had a bit of luck here because I met by chance in a pub a young man who turned out to be a most gifted artist and also, unusual for an artist so talented, he was most generous with his gift. His speciality was painting trains, cars and, yes, aircraft, and so I had struck gold! Contrary to my principles, I gladly accepted when, over the period of our friendship, he offered me several tips on drawing aircraft, which helped me to improve. Despite his help, I still needed to follow the same procedure in daubing an aircraft as I used with a ship at sea, so I would paint the sky around the aircraft, impinging the paint on the fuselage or wings where necessary, until the thing looked absolutely right.

Now I have something vital to tell you about painting a picture of an aeroplane flying. It has to be actually flying! Please don't put the book down. I am not just stating the obvious, I am trying to inform you of the main difficulty in aviation painting. There are many paintings of an aircraft apparently flying against a nice-looking background sky and, if you have never flown an aircraft or been part of a real aircrew, then you might regard the painting as absolutely super. But is it? The great difficulty for an aviation artist is to impart to the viewer the feeling that the aeroplane is actually flying. With some aviation paintings, the longer you look at them the more you begin to wonder what that unreal lump of cigar-shaped metal is doing apparently up there in a sky. However beautifully the aeroplane itself is painted, if it does not integrate with the sky, you will feel that it is about to go fluttering down out of the bottom of the canvas. If the painting is in acrylic, which has that lurid and poster-like effect, then almost certainly the aircraft will look unreal. To a pilot or any aircrew it is unlikely that an acrylic-painted aircraft would appear to be really flying. How then to achieve in paint the effect of flight?

I believe that painting an aircraft in watercolour, that wonderful sensitive medium, may produce the right result naturally. But I don't really know, do I, because the water medium is too difficult for me to even try. Such a pity as such aviation paintings in watercolour I have seen, have nearly all been good and with a sense of reality about them. But I stick to the precept of my Mentor, Winston Churchill, in his book Painting as a Pastime:

La peinture à l'huile
Est bien difficile,
Mais c'est beaucoup plus beau
Que la peinture à l'eau.

And so back we go to our oats, which is daubing in oil. The ability I found to paint aeroplanes, which properly appear to be flying in their environment of the clouds, was not some secret formula I discovered. No, the means of achieving reality seems to come naturally and normally with keeping the same palette colours throughout the picture, just as I wrote earlier for landscapes and seascapes. This means that the basic colours, which form your grey for the sky, are the same as those within and part of your aircraft. Thus your aircraft is truly integrated with the clouds and sky around it and is truly flying in its natural environment. New daubers don't have to worry therefore about how to make aircraft look as if it is really flying, I believe they need only follow my earlier tips on mixing the palette and essentially using those mixed colours throughout the entire painting including, of course, the aircraft itself. I would like to help new daubers in drawing the aircraft itself but I don't have the ability to do so.

A DAUBER'S PROGRESS

Daubing **figures** I find very difficult because of my lack of drawing ability and trying to copy a photograph of children on a beach, for instance, doesn't serve either, simply because I am unable to copy. Anyway, beware of photographing children on a beach for artistic purposes or you may have a manic Mum after you, such is the effect of our unbalanced Press. My method of daubing figures, which may be of help to other daubers with a similar lack of draughtsmanship, is as follows. First I complete the picture of the beach, the sea and rocks and wait for it to dry. Then, with a thin piece of charcoal, I experiment with little stick figures until I get their basic posture right for whatever they are doing. It is important to keep the figures in the picture reasonably distant so that their size on the canvas is no more than, say, two inches. The next stage, when the postures in charcoal are as you want, is to paint delicately (for a change!) over the little sticks with a very thin brush using your dark grey from the palette. It is best to let that dry again, if you can be patient, before delicately you re-paint over the stick figures using flesh-tinted cool grey and colours for the clothes. I always start with the figure's bottom from which I do the legs and secondly the angle of the back and so to the head, whose position is most vital. Try it and see.

Selling the daubs and all that

Once you are well into the swing of daubing and have become better at it, you will find three very good reasons for selling your pictures, if you can. The primary reason why all artists and all daubers ardently want to sell their work is the gigantic thrill it gives them when their picture is sold. Just think of it. There you stand facing the wide expanse of a bare white canvas, whereupon from out of your own mind and applying the three Ms, you conjure up a lovely picture and then contrive to transpose it by a process of daubing on to what had been a barren field. Your picture is seen by a stranger, a friend or even a gallery owner, it doesn't matter which, and they want to buy it. It is a dream come true. It is the thrill of a lifetime and don't any Artist or dauber dare tell me that they are not interested in selling their paintings because to do so is bare-faced fibbing (to use a nice word for it).

The second reason for selling is that, unless you are intending to produce only an occasional daub, painting in oils can be expensive in materials if you are not economically careful, and you will need to recover your costs.

Thirdly, because you so enjoy daubing, you will accumulate masses of the completed pictures which you will need to be rid of, and to sell them is the best, if not the easiest, means of doing so.

A DAUBER'S PROGRESS

You can give your daubs away, of course, and I did so once but rarely again because I found my first gift had been hung in the lavatory. I was hurt and have been mean about them ever since.

I wouldn't advise you to become interested in the various Royal Societies and Academies which abound in the art world, as I believe that they have rather lost their way and sense of purpose. They were surely intended to form a nucleus of the very best artists in Britain who would exhibit now and then to show the British people and the world the high standard our best could produce. In fact, as it seems to me, these Societies tend to have opened their membership to all sorts of artists who are not of a high standard. There is little point therefore in spending money on membership, particularly since often the paintings don't sell well at their exhibitions, even though their prices are reasonably low. I have never found the need to bother with them.

There is little to be gained by approaching the big well-known galleries because, although I have by chance broken into them a couple of times, they deal only with professional Artists of a known following and reputation with whom they usually have contracts for a specified number of paintings.

And so for your sales, you may have to rely largely on the smaller art galleries. I suggest that it is sensible to choose those galleries who trade in the area of your type of subject, For example, I would use galleries in seaside Weymouth, Salcombe, Tenby, Watchet and North Devon for my seascapes while galleries in small towns and cities are usually best for landscapes.

The first step you have to take is to confront the owner of the small gallery and there is nearly always an amusing pattern of ritualistic behaviour in this initial confrontation. Sometimes the owner may even be an artist and know a good daub or painting when he or she sees one. But more likely the owner has only a vague understanding about the quality of any painting and his or her concern therefore is to discover your artistic background and reputation and to find out whether you have sold paintings and where.

The method I learned to use for coping with these gallery people was initially to leave my daub behind in the car and wander round the gallery examining the paintings. Soon the owner would come simpering up to enquire if he could be of help, to which I would reply that I was an Artist and was interested to see if his gallery was suitable for my standard and style of painting. Now that we both knew what we were at, so to speak, the ritual confrontation would start and there we would be dancing and mentally fencing with each other around the middle of the gallery floor with, by this time, my daub up on an easel for inspection. You are desperate for the wretched man or woman to take the damn daub and put it up for sale and so you imply how good an Artist you are and how many paintings you have sold and where, and you might even let slip a mention of the Ulster Academy. Whether your daub is any good or not doesn't come into the gallery owner's consideration as yet. Because he or she, on the other hand, is desperately nervous of missing a trick and that maybe your daub is in reality a super painting and might, with others like it, make him or her a bomb of profit. The description of that situation is not my imagination working, by the way, I have been through it so many times. Anyway, let's say the owner agrees to take your daubs on trial, the next major contract term to agree is the commission for the gallery. This will be between 33% and 55% dependant as a rough rule on how near to London is the gallery. In any case, you don't argue.

But please don't be daunted by these gallery people or put off in any way by them because they are only sales people and few of them know about art.

I disliked that gallery procedure so much that, in a short while, I arranged to sell most of my daubs by organising my own exhibitions at appropriate places, such as a gallery or a museum. Sometimes it was an advantage to share an exhibition and the costs and work of it with a fellow artist or dauber. Altogether, during my retirement years, I have held nine such exhibitions. Arising from sales at these exhibitions, I became better known and in recent years my daubs have been commissioned by clubs or by individuals. This is a gentlemanly way of being a dauber and, when asked if I will take a commission, I do my best to appear calm and to disguise my delight before discussing seriously what type of daub is required. It is fascinating trying to understand what the customer wants and then transposing it on to the canvas. And, best of all, what you earn you get without paying half of it to a gallery!

Joyful retirement

I may have given the impression in these notes on DIY daubing that I have been at it ever since I started in 1956 at the age of thirty-four. In fact it wasn't like that at all because in about 1960 I was given a desk to fly instead of an aircraft. The resulting workload and necessity for much foreign travel as a passenger meant I had to stop daubing entirely until I retired twenty-five years later. And how wonderful it was when I did retire to take up daubing again.

On retirement, I started to paint rather tentatively wondering whether I would be able to do anything worthwhile because, after all, it would be expensive to buy all the materials and then find that I was no good at it. So it was until Heather, my dear wife, gave me a right wigging and reminded me that daubing had always been my pleasure to do and it simply didn't matter a damn whether I was any good at it or not. Having been put into the right frame of mind, I re-started in earnest and soon had two or three canvases going, splodging the paint happily on all of them. The main point for fellow daubers to remember when they retire is that daubing is not a skill ever to be lost because, as I have tried to indicate all along, there isn't a lot of actual skill to it anyway. But each picture does require you to think about it and to use both your memory and imagination. What better mental activity could there be for a retired person? And above all, there is always the sheer joy of doing it.

Another good factor about daubing in retirement is that it gives you a reason to travel affordable distances, instead of bumbling aimlessly about in the car. In my case we had retired to Ross-on-Wye, which was not only in a beautiful area, but was close to the border of Wales where I hoped to find the wilder and more mountainous type of country I needed for my sort of daubing. Also for seascapes, I hoped to find some rocky coastal areas because, rather as I had done at sea in a carrier, I liked to sit on a rocky ledge just watching the sea swirling and smashing around the rocks below. I wasn't disappointed because I found Wales be every bit as beautiful and in parts as wild as it was said to be. Yet though it had remote areas of country it was different to the lonely and mystic land I had found previously on the west coast of Ireland. In Wales, even around most of the rugged mountains, there were good roads and the valleys were more cultivated with trees and attractive villages. Yet, as well as beautiful valleys with a typical groups of small cottages to paint, there were other more desolate-looking, stony and arid areas of Wales to satisfy my urge to produce dramatic daubs with lovely great skies above the mountains.

The freedom of retirement and a couple of small pensions enabled my wife and me to explore either the country or the coast of South Wales, staying for a night at small hotels or pubs, and so to return to Ross with my mind full of potential daubs. After a time, we made a practice of staying in Tenby where we could enjoy the beach scenes but also use it as a base for exploring the wilder areas of mid-Wales. An ordinary car was not much good for tackling the type of rocky and stony country or coast where we wanted to be for daubing and so, in due course, we bought an ugly Japanese thing with big wheels and lots of gears, which was capable almost of taking us up a mountain. The pleasure and fun of daubing was all very well but the number of daubs and the cost of doing them was mounting and so, of necessity, we also had to travel to art galleries in the north and south of Devon, in Somerset, Dorset, the Cotswolds and in South Wales while hoping that these galleries would take my daubs to sell. In fact, most of the galleries did so but it was not easy, as I have written above.

Envoi

Forgive me for having written all that guff about selling my daubs but, if you would look at it in the context of my two first attempts at painting, compared with later daubs, it has the purpose of encouraging new daubers that they can do the same. I hope to show how, from our small beginnings as daubers, we can all come to be recognised as, dare I use the word, Artists. But please remember that the main reason for daubing is the sheer pleasure and joy of doing it.

Daubing as I have described it is of great benefit if, in old age, you should become partially blind as I have. My method of daubing, plonking the paint on to the canvas without too much detail, lends itself perfectly to a blind condition. Hence I have arranged to hold my final exhibition to celebrate my ninetieth birthday.

A DAUBER'S PROGRESS

These are pictures painted by Hank from 1956 to 1960 while in Ireland. He did no daubing from 1960 to 1985.

1. The Cottage
2. The Seascape
3. Passing the headland, 22 x 18 inches
4. View of Copeland Island, 28 x 24 inches, first commission.
5. Trawler at sea, 24 x 28
6. Boy sailing *Velindra*, 22 x 18
7. Deep water rock
8. Seafire in the clouds
9. Valley among the Twelve Pins
10. On passage to fishing grounds

The following are some of the pictures Hank painted after 1985 when he re-started. In all over 250 daubs were sold or commissioned at prices sufficient to cover their costs.

11. Offshore rocks, 18 x 14 inches
12. Peeping Janes, 22 x 16 inches
13. A lee shore, 22 x 16 inches
14. Country farm in Herefordshire, 18 x 12 inches
15. Envious boys, 22 x 16 inches
16. Trawler on passage to fishing grounds, 24 x 18 inches
17. Kite flying on the beach, 18 x 14 inches
18. Landing the village stores on a Devon beach, 28 x 20 inches. Commissioned by Mr Tom Gover

19. Welsh mountains, 16 x 12 inches
20. Atop the Brecons, 16 x 12 inches (a 'Blinder')
21. Book cover commissioned by Airlife Publishing, 1995, for *Up in Harm's Way* by Commander R M Crosley, DSC and Bar, RN
22. Children on the beach
23. Book illustration for a short story, 22 x 18 inches
24. Chasing the Condor, 30 x 24 inches.
    Commissioned by Wardroom, RNAS Yeovilton.
25. Corsairs strafing a Japanese airfield, 32 x 28 inches. Commissioned by Wardroom, RNAS Yeovilton.
26. Corsairs returning from patrol to land on HMS *Colossus*, 30 x 24 inches
27. Lt Gray VC, DSC, takes off with his flight of Corsairs from HMS *Victorious*, 36 x 28 inches. Exhibited at Christie's in London and purchased by the Victory Services Club
28. Making more sail, 28 x 24 inches. Commissioned by Mr Don Pople
29. HMS *Speedy* returns to Falmouth. Commissioned by Mr Chris Rouse
30. Caught by the French. Commissioned by Mr John Rogers
31. Red kites over the Brecons, 22 x 18 inches
32. 'Enemy leaving harbour', HMS *Pickle* reports to Nelson before Trafalgar.
    Commissioned by the Bath and County Club

A DAUBER'S PROGRESS

1956 to 1960

1. The Cottage
2. The Seascape

3. Passing the Headland
4. View of Copeland Island

5. Trawler at Sea
6. Boy sailing *Velindra*

7. Deep water rock
8. Seafire in the clouds

9. Valley among the Twelve Pins
10. On passage to fishing grounds

1985 to 2012

11. Offshore rocks
12. Peeping Janes

13. A lee shore
14. Country farm in Herefordshire

15. Envious boys
16. Trawler on passage to fishing grounds

17. Kite flying on the beach
18. Landing the village stores on a Devon beach

19. Welsh mountains
20. Atop the Brecons

21. Book cover commissioned by Airlife Publishing
22. Children on the beach

23. Book illustration for a short story
24. Chasing the Condor

25. Corsairs strafing a Japanese airfield
26. Corsairs returning from patrol to land on HMS
   Colossus

27. Lt Gray VC, DSC, takes off with his flight of
    Corsairs from HMS *Victorious*
28. Making more sail

29. HMS *Speedy* returns to Falmouth
30. Caught by the French

31. Red kites over the Brecons
32. HMS *Pickle* reports to Nelson before Trafalgar